A PLEA FOR VEGETARIANISM

AND OTHER ESSAYS

H. S. SALT

Published by Left of Brain Books

ISBN 978-1-396-31832-0

First Edition

Table of Contents

"I have no doubt that it is a part of the destiny of the human race, in its gradual improvement, to leave off eating animals, as surely as the savage tribes have left off eating each other, when they came in contact with the more civilised."

H. D. THOREAU

PREFATORY NOTE.

1

Two of the following Essays, *viz.*, Nos. I. and VI., are reprinted from *Time* for February, 1883, and January, 1886. The rest have appeared at different times in the pages of the *Food Reform Magazine*, the *Dietetic Reformer*, and the Vegetarian Society's *Annual*.

A PLEA FOR VEGETARIANISM.

I must preface this essay by the confession that I am myself a Vegetarian, and that I mean to say all the good I can of the principles of Vegetarianism. This is rather a formidable admission to, make, for a Vegetarian is still regarded, in ordinary society, as little better than a madman, and may consider himself lucky if he has no worse epithets applied to him than humanitarian, sentimentalist, crotchet-monger, fanatic, and the like. A man who leaves off eating flesh will soon find that his friends and acquaintances look on him with strange and wondering eyes; his life is invested with a mysterious interest; his death is an event which is regarded as by no means distant or improbable. Some of his friends, who take a graver view of such dietetic vagaries, feel it to be their duty to warn him boldly and explicitly that he will undoubtedly die in a short time unless he amends his ways. Others content themselves with the more cautious assertion that he is undermining his health by slow degrees, and will inevitably fall a victim to the first severe attack of illness that may befall him. Others, again, are of opinion that though his bodily health may not suffer, yet his mental powers will be sapped by a fleshless diet, and he will soon sink into a state of hopeless idiocy and imbecility. On the other hand, there are some who readily admit the possibility of living without meat, but profess themselves, with a pitying smile of superior intelligence, utterly unable to imagine any reason for such abstinence.

In spite of these somewhat discouraging reflections, I think it will be worth our while to inquire if there be really such great absurdity in the idea of not eating flesh, or if it be possible that the Vegetarians have reason on their side, and that the present movement in favour of a reformed diet may contain the germ of an important change. However that may be, it can do no harm to my readers if they hear what can be said in favour of Vegetarianism; then, if they are not persuaded to adopt a fleshless diet, they will have a clear conscience, and be able to enjoy their beef and mutton all the more afterwards.

The first and most obvious advantage of a vegetarian diet is its economy. Flesh-meat is so much more expensive than cereals and vegetable products, that it must be accounted very extravagant and unbusinesslike to use it as a common article of food, unless, as is generally believed, its superior quality compensates in the long run for its dearness. But if Vegetarians find that they live in perfect health without meat, would they not be somewhat deficient in common-sense if they did not make the most of their pecuniary advantage? The humanitarians, sentimentalists, crotchet-mongers, and fanatics have therefore, at least, one point in their favour—the cost of their food is far less than that of the shrewd flesh-eater. I mention this point first as being the most plain and indisputable, not necessarily the most important; yet that it is also of great importance will scarcely be denied, in a country whose food supply is yearly becoming a matter of greater difficulty, and where thousands of people are in a state of abject poverty and want. Even in well-to-do households the price of meat is a source of constant complaint and vexation to the prudent housewife; yet she would laugh to scorn the bare idea of living without flesh, and, if she has ever thought of Vegetarianism, has thought of it only as an impious absurdity and dangerous hallucination of modern times, to be classed with Mormonism, Spiritualism, Anglo-Israelism, Socialism, and possibly Atheism itself. "What sort of a religion must that be?" was the remark of an old and faithful servant when she heard that her former master had become a Vegetarian—a remark typical of the attitude of society towards the Vegetarian movement.

Secondly: Is it not equally unquestionable that it is both more humane, and what, for want of a comprehensive word, I must call more "æsthetic," not to slaughter animals for food, unless it be really necessary to do so? If it can be shown that men can live equally well without flesh-food, or, rather, unless it can be shown that the contrary is the case (for the burden of proof must always rest with those who take on themselves the responsibility of wholesale slaughter), it must surely seem unjustifiable, on the score of humanity, to breed and kill animals for merely culinary purposes.

Cæteris paribus, there is therefore a moral advantage in a vegetarian diet; and the humanitarians and sentimentalists are only fulfilling a real duty in abstaining from animal food, if experience has shown it to be in their case unnecessary. And, if we assume for a moment that a fleshless diet is practicable, how cruel to animals, and how degrading to men, is the institution of the slaughter-house! Having no wish to dwell on what is morbid and unpleasant, I shall not pain the feelings of my readers by harping on the sufferings which their victims undergo, but shall content myself with remarking that those good people are mistaken who imagine that the slaughter of animals is painless and merciful. A society has lately been instituted (not by Vegetarians) with the object of introducing into our slaughter-houses more humane and sanitary methods of procedure. The mere existence of such a society is a proof that the system is not free from cruelty; but if anyone wishes for further proof, he has only to read, if he has nerve enough to do so, the account which the society has published of the present system of slaughtering.

But, as I said before, the practice of flesh-eating is not only cruel towards animals, but degrading to men—to those, at least, who have eyes to see, and ears to hear, the teaching of morality and good taste. A truly "æsthetic" eye would surely be shocked by the horrible display of carcases with which our butchers are wont to bedeck their shops; and it is indeed a strange predilection that induces even ladies to go in person to the market to buy their "butchers' meat," as that article is euphemistically entitled, and to ask anxiously the important question, "when was it killed?" A truly "æsthetic" ear would hardly be charmed by the lowing of cattle and bleating of sheep when they are driven hurriedly down our streets by an individual dressed in blue. A truly "æsthetic" palate and a truly "æsthetic" nose (if there be "æstheticism" in these senses) could hardly relish the flavour of "meat," however artfully mitigated and concealed by the skill of the cook. The greatest and most unerring argument in favour of Vegetarianism is, to my mind, the utter absence of "good taste" in flesh-eating, which is revolting to all the higher instincts of the human mind. "Methinks at meals some odd thoughts might intrude," says Byron; and if they do not intrude in most cases, it is only another proof of the wellnigh insuperable power of custom and prejudice.

It appears, then, that both on economic and moral grounds there are certain very distinct advantages in a vegetarian diet, provided only that such a diet can be shown to be physically practicable. This is, in reality, the cardinal point of the whole controversy; and we accordingly find that the possibility, or, at any rate, the advisability of Vegetarianism on physical grounds is most pertinaciously denied. The popular idea is, of course, that meat is the only food which gives strength, and that Vegetarianism is wellnigh impossible. "Don't you feel very weak?" is generally the first question asked of a Vegetarian, by a new friend or acquaintance; and if we press for a clearer explanation of this vague belief in the strength-giving qualities of meat, we find that it is composed of two distinct and sometimes contradictory notions—first, that meat is necessary to support bodily strength; secondly, that mental work cannot be done without it. "Vegetarianism," says one, "may be all very well for the rich and indolent, but the hard-working man must have his meat." "The labouring classes," says another, "may doubtless perform their merely bodily work on a vegetarian diet, but those who have to work with their minds need a more stimulating diet." The Vegetarian thus finds himself placed between Scylla and Charybdis, but neither argument, when carefully examined, will be found to be very formidable. To prove that the former is quite fallacious, one need only refer to the undeniable fact that in all countries the mass of the peasantry live in robust health without flesh-meat, for the simple reason that they cannot afford to get it. The latter supposition, for it is nothing more, that the intellectual classes stand in special need of flesh-meat, is equally unfortunate, in face of the positive evidence of Vegetarians that they can do their mental work as well, or better, without meat; and of the well-known fact that great writers have usually eaten little or no flesh-meat, especially when engaged on any literary work. The belief that meat alone can give strength may therefore be dismissed as a mere error, resulting from prejudice or thoughtlessness.

The objection of chemists and medical men to a vegetarian diet is based rather on the belief that meat is the most convenient form of food: they admit that Vegetarianism is possible, but deny that it is advisable: a vegetarian diet may be well enough, but a mixed diet is preferable. Such was the line of argument taken up by the scientific champions of flesh-eating, in the controversy on the "Great Food Question," to which a good deal of space was devoted a few months ago (1882) in the columns of the *Echo*. It is, of course, impossible for Vegetarians to prove to demonstration that such a theory is wrong; but it should be observed that it is a theory only: all the practical evidence that can be obtained goes to indicate that abstinence from flesh-food causes no physical deterioration, but rather the reverse. Indeed, those who have themselves made practical trial of Vegetarianism, although perhaps devoid of any technical knowledge of the digestive organs, cannot but smile at the arbitrary assertions and objections of learned men; nor can they be much interested by the information that flesh-meat is chemically superior, when they happen to have learnt by experience that they are much better without it. They adopt a rough-and-ready style of reasoning which is very disturbing to scientific minds; their boldness is "magnificent, but it is not war." They are like Diogenes, who, when learned men were demonstrating by subtle and flawless argument "that motion is impossible," was provoking enough to rise from his seat and move about. In short, it is abundantly evident that the "Great Food Question," whatever its ultimate solution may be, is not one that will be settled by the authority of chemists and physicians. *Quot homines, tot sententiæ.* We Vegetarians have no wish, on our part, to be dogmatic and interfering; but with regard to the physical aspect of Vegetarianism, which, as I said before, is the cardinal point of the whole question, we are at least justified by the facts of the case in asserting this much. There is overwhelming proof that Vegetarianism is possible; there is an utter absence of proof that it is in any way detrimental to perfect health. It is, therefore, at least worthy of more serious consideration than it has yet received; before it is ridiculed and condemned it should at least be tried.

But it must not be supposed that Vegetarians rely solely on personal experience and empirical proof—they, too, can appeal with confidence to the teaching of science and physiology. The fact that the structure of the human body is wholly unlike that of the carnivora, and that the apes, who are nearest akin to us in the animal world, are frugivorous, is a somewhat strong indication that flesh is not the natural food of mankind. And if it be said that man, unlike other creatures, is omnivorous, and has therefore to seek not what is "natural," but what is best, then I readily accept the challenge, and reply that there is a strong concurrence of proof, on economic, moral, and physical grounds, that a vegetarian diet is the most suitable and beneficial. Among various advantages, it has one inestimable blessing; it is less stimulating than flesh-food, while it is equally nutritious. If people could only realise how much vice and violence is caused by over-stimulating food, they would soon recognise the importance of a non-stimulating diet. On the other hand, if they would only remember how much misery is caused by a lack of nutritious food, they would welcome a diet-system which, by its vast economic saving, would bring within our reach an abundance of cheap and wholesome nutriment. From whichever point one may regard this question, utilitarian or moral, it will appear more and more marvellous that men should persist in squandering their money and repressing their finest moral impulses, in order to supply themselves with the costly food which they stupidly imagine to be necessary for their physical health.

In addition to the serious arguments brought forward by the scientific opponents of Vegetarianism, there are, of course, many minor objections which are constantly cropping up when the subject is discussed in ordinary conversation, all of them more or less fallacious, and some exceptionally remarkable for the curious insight they give one into the mental state of those who advance them. Many and many a time have I been begged to explain "what would become of the animals" under a vegetarian *régime*, fears being sometimes expressed that they would drive mankind from off the face of the earth, at other times that they would themselves perish miserably in utter want and destitution! Many and many a time have I been reminded, not as a joke, but as a serious argument, that animals were "sent" us as food! I have no space here to notice these and similar difficulties; and, in truth, it is but a thankless task to answer them at any time, for they are hydra-headed monsters, and spring up as fast as one can cut them down. It is a mournful fact that when people have no wish to understand a thing, they can generally contrive to misunderstand it; and the hopelessness of pleading with those who will not or cannot comprehend is one of the first lessons learnt by Food Reformers, as, indeed, by reformers of all kinds. I once heard of a physician, of some local repute, who not only condemned the principles of Vegetarianism, but professed himself entirely unaware of the existence of Vegetarians. When informed that such persons do undoubtedly exist, he persisted in regarding them as impostors who maintained a spurious reputation by artifices such as those attributed to Doctor Tanner, or the "Welsh fasting girl," and gravely inquired, "Are you sure they do not eat meat *by night?*"

It has been the unambitious object of this paper to show that Vegetarianism is worth more serious consideration than this, and that it is not a mere foolish craze and hallucination. When charged with fanaticism and infatuation, the Vegetarian may well retort, in the words of Hamlet—

Ecstasy!
My pulse, as yours, doth temperately keep time,
And makes as healthful music. It is not madness
That I have uttered: bring me to the test.

To bring a question to the test is, however, a process which to most people is particularly disagreeable. They greatly prefer the easier and more expeditious method of shaping their ideas in accordance with the time-honoured traditions of custom and "society;" and hence, on the subject of food, they cling firmly to the notion that the roast beef of England is the *summum bonum* of dietetic aspiration. I believe that time will prove this to be a fallacy, and that future and wiser generations will look back with amazement on the habit of flesh-eating as a strange relic of ignorance and barbarism.

MORALITY IN DIET.

It is strange that, among the many important subjects which at this time are demanding investigation from every thoughtful man, Vegetarianism has not attracted more general attention. For, though it cannot be classed among those vexed "questions of the day" which occupy the time of Parliament and agitate the surface of party politics, yet it may safely be asserted that there is no matter which more truly deserves full and patient inquiry than this question of diet, connected as it is with the deep underlying problems—How to live. How to improve and elevate, mentally and bodily, the lives of our fellow-countrymen. In all ages, from the days of Pythagoras to the days of Shelley, Vegetarianism has had its prophets and apostles; but they have for the most part stood alone and isolated, solitary lights amidst almost universal darkness. Now, at last, in this progressive age, when the morality of life is more widely studied, and the laws of health and economy are better understood, earnest and hard-working men should be induced at least to give fair and unprejudiced examination to a system which claims to be at once most *moral*, most *wholesome*, and most *economical*. For these are the three great advantages which the Vegetarian believes his way of living to possess; these are the three chief aspects under which Vegetarianism may be viewed; and surely, amidst all the clamour and din of conflicting theories and creeds, it is right that the voice of Vegetarianism should be heard, and that the cruelty and wastefulness of the system of flesh-eating should not be allowed to pass unchallenged. Obviously the same arguments will not have like weight with all; for while to the poorer classes it is the economic advantage of Vegetarianism that is of most pressing and immediate importance, to wealthier and more educated people the moral side of the question needs to be most forcibly stated. It is of this last that I now speak. My object is to show that only a bloodless diet is defensible on moral grounds.

There is a passage in Mr. Ruskin's works, where it is declared that a criterion of the morality of an action may be found in song, Actions are morally beautiful in proportion to their capability of becoming the subject of song. This is a standard from which no Vegetarian will ever shrink, which no flesh-eater will ever dare to accept. The fruits and cereals of a vegetarian meal might well find mention in the purest and most delicate poem. Could the same be said of the repast of a flesh-eater? What are the dainties which Porphyro, in Keats's "Eve of St. Agnes," heaps "with glowing hand" for his love, "in the retired quiet of the night"? They are "candied apple, quince, and plum, and gourd, manna and dates," and other "delicates" which would rejoice the soul of a Vegetarian. What would have been the effect on the poem, if instead of these, he had heaped beef-steaks and mutton-chops? And why is it that the mere idea of such a change is at once disgusting and ridiculous? Again, would it not be admitted on all hands that fruits and herbs and corn would be a right and natural subject for the skill of a vegetarian poet? Yet what should we think, if some enthusiastic flesh-eater were to give vent to the poetry of his feelings in a "Song of the Slaughter-house," or "Ballads of the Butcher"? And why is it that, while the one subject would be innocent and elevating, the other would be loathsome and degrading?

This criterion, however, may be considered too fanciful, if we carry it to its logical conclusion. So we will not ask the supporters of the present system to *sing* of such subjects: we will merely beg of them to *think*. For thought is surely the best and truest standard by which we may distinguish the right from the wrong. That action and system are the best which can best stand the scrutiny of thought. We will therefore venture to think about our diet, even though it be at the risk of shocking delicate-minded ladies and gentlemen, who vote it impolite and disgusting to refer to such matters as the slaughter of animals, and brand all such inquiry with the epithet "morbid," or "sentimental." We will cease to regard "beef," and "mutton," and "pork" as lifeless articles of food, but will remember that they have a close connection with living oxen, and sheep, and swine. We will request those who perpetuate the butcher's trade by eating flesh-meat to consider seriously what that trade is. Why is the very name *butcher* proverbial? Why is the slaughter-house unmentionable at polite dinner-tables? If the system of flesh-eating is defensible, why must its method of supply be concealed from all thought or reference? The obvious answer is that this trade is a degrading one, and not only socially but morally degrading. There are many occupations which gentlemen, for social and conventional reasons, would be ashamed to practise, such as shoe-blacking and chimney-sweeping. Yet there is no real or moral degradation in these, such as there is in the wanton slaughter of innocent animals. If our sweeps and shoe-blacks were suddenly to go on strike, and we were compelled to do such work for ourselves, a wise man, however refined, would never be ashamed to soil his hand with soot or blacking, But if, through a similar emergency, he lost the services of his butcher, he might well think twice before he polluted himself with blood.

If, then, it be a degrading occupation to kill animals, how can the habit of eating them be other than degrading? If we condemn the ignorant and brutal butcher who supplies the flesh, how can we acquit the refined ladies and gentlemen who demand it? Thoughtlessness alone enables people to endure such a system. From infancy they are taught to ignore what "meat" really is; until they hardly think of oxen and sheep in connection with beef and mutton.

And now contrast with this diet the life of a Vegetarian. Here there is no need of secrecy and sophistry to make the meal palatable, for the history of beans and lentils is not a record of blood and suffering, and we are not obliged to dismiss all thought as to the origin of our food, lest we should awaken reminiscences of the filth of the pigsty and the butchery of the shambles. There is nothing to conceal, for there is nothing to be ashamed of. It is the only diet which is entirely in keeping with the highest moral instincts of the most intellectual mind.

There are also indirect advantages in Vegetarianism, which can hardly fail to commend it to all those who know the value of temperance, both in food and drink. It is in general closely connected with frugality and simplicity of taste: with teetotalism it is specially allied, for moderation in drink is the natural result of moderation in food, and it is an undoubted fact that the craving for alcohol is enormously lessened by a vegetarian diet.

Here, however, it may perhaps be objected, that, although Vegetarianism may be desirable on abstract grounds of morality and good taste, nevertheless flesh-eating is, for physical reasons, a practical necessity of nature, and, being natural, cannot be immoral. This, of course, belongs rather to the physical than the moral question; and it remains for those who have satisfied themselves that Vegetarianism is desirable to determine further whether it is practicable. It is sufficient here to indicate the fact that medical men are not only not infallible, but liable to all the prejudices that affect the unprofessional mind; so that would be Vegetarians need not be greatly alarmed by the stock arguments which are regularly produced by doctors, cooks, relatives, and other well-meaning persons, in the way of solemn warning and advice. The Vegetarian is assured that the impossibility of such a diet for man is clearly demonstrated by the formation of the teeth, and other structural evidence. Some nations and individuals may contrive to live on vegetable food, in spite of these physical hindrances; but at any rate in northern climates a flesh diet is, necessary, for the sake of heat. And if some obstinate people even here persist in living in perfect health without animal food, still it is absolutely certain (and this is the final resource, the great irrefragable dogma of the flesh-eater) that meat is necessary to foster intellectual vigour, even where physical strength may be supported without it.

And thus the fellow-countrymen of Shelley are led to believe that the finest work cannot be done without the grossest food; and that while man's mortal body may be nourished on a pure and bloodless diet, it is the intellect—the spark that kindles the fire of poetry, music, science, and the arts—it is the intellect which requires to be fed on the loathsome carcases of slaughtered sheep and bullocks!

Let us, therefore, one and all, undismayed by sonorous warnings and dogmatic assertions, quietly and fearlessly ask our own consciences if the present system of diet is morally right and defensible; and if the answer be, as I have attempted to prove it must be, in the negative, let us not shrink from the consequent duty of attempting a reform. The experience of those who have honestly and seriously made trial of Vegetarianism gives overwhelming testimony in its favour. Its economical advantage is indisputably great; not less conspicuous, to those who make practical proof for themselves, is its physical superiority, insuring, as it does, a simpler, healthier, more enjoyable manner of life, and affording immunity, as Vegetarians very plausibly assert, from many of our worst diseases and epidemics.

The progress of all reforms is slow; and in the question of diet, as in all others, a national error takes centuries, as Sydney Smith has observed, "to display the full bloom of its imbecility"; yet a Vegetarian, without being over sanguine, may well comfort himself with the reflection that, in the case of flesh-eating, these conditions have now been amply fulfilled, and that the outlook is therefore not entirely devoid of encouragement. Centuries have passed; we see our upper classes rioting in degrading wastefulness, while our lower classes are sunk in degrading want, and both alike the victims of degrading, because unnecessary, disease.[1] The failure of our diet system is complete; the bloom of its imbecility is displayed for all eyes to see. Is it too much to hope that we may soon cease to be blinded by prejudice and custom, and that the civilised world may, before many generations have passed, adopt the opinion of the philanthropist Howard, founded on a life-time of experience and observation? "I am fully persuaded as to the health of our bodies, that herbs and fruits will sustain nature in every respect far beyond the best flesh."

---

[1] "I have come to the conclusion that a proportion, amounting at least to more than one-half of the disease which embitters the middle and latter part of life among the middle and upper classes of the population, is due to avoidable errors in diet" (Sir Henry Thompson on "Diet," *Nineteenth Century*, May, 1885). On the other hand, eminent authorities have told us that the London poor suffer mainly from one disease—starvation.

GOOD TASTE IN DIET.

It is a remarkable and lamentable fact that the movement in favour of Food Reform finds but few supporters among the classes known as "æsthetic" and "artistic;" among those, in short, who pride themselves on their so-called "good taste," and who might, therefore, have been especially looked to for favour and sympathy. For, setting aside for the present all considerations of morality and gentleness, I maintain that there are just as glaring faults of bad taste visible in our system of diet as in our dress, or furniture, or general household arrangements, all of which have been very severely and very properly criticised by the æsthetic school. How foolish and inconsistent it is to be vastly fastidious about the manner in which one's food is served up, and at the same time to be totally indifferent as regards the quality, from an æsthetic view, of the food itself! The highest art may be apparent in the decoration and arrangement of the table, but, if the food be gross in taste and smell, the result can hardly be gratifying to the truly æsthetic mind.

But, it may be asked, is it a fact that flesh-food is gross in taste and smell? One of the commonest objections of flesh-eaters to the reformed diet is that flesh-meat is "nice," and the guests at an æsthetic dinner-table have presumably no sort of suspicion that they are eating anything which is not "high art." Of course dietetic taste, like all other taste, is relative and subjective; there is no absolute criterion of "good taste," but each man must decide for himself what he considers "nice." It is therefore impossible to *prove* the superiority of the reformed diet, or to convince flesh-eaters that their taste is not immaculate. We can only trust to the results of experience, and the good taste which is gradually brought about by culture and education. All Vegetarians will emphatically deny that flesh-food is nice, and will assert that only a depraved and uncultivated taste can relish it; and if our æsthetic friends will give the matter a little serious consideration, they will very soon find themselves arriving at the same conclusion.

So far I have used the word *æstheticism* as merely equivalent to the actual perception by the senses, a meaning to which its modern votaries seem to wish to restrict it. But in real truth it cannot be thus limited, at any rate in dietetic questions, for we cannot wholly exclude the consideration of the origin of our food. However gratifying our flesh-meat may be to our immediate taste (a very gross and uncultured taste, as I have attempted to show), we cannot altogether forget its extremely unpleasant antecedents. However artistic the arrangement of the dinner-table, however immaculate the table-cloth and faultless the dinner-service, the disagreeable thought must surely sometimes occur to the artistic mind that the beef was once an ox, the mutton was once a sheep, the veal was once a calf, and the pork was once a pig. We may scrupulously make clean the outside of the cup and platter, but the recollection of the state of their interior will nevertheless cause some disquietude to our æsthetic repose. In fact, though we may well be thankful for any reaction against the gross materialism and vulgarity of modern society, it may be doubted whether any class can be truly æsthetic which does not recognise in its creed the supreme importance of gentleness and humanity. The man who keenly sympathises with the suffering of dumb animals has a more truly æsthetic mind than many of our modern connoisseurs of "high art" who are inexpressibly pained by the sight of an ugly house or an inartistic piece of furniture, while they view with entire equanimity a system of diet which necessitates the very ugly trade of the butcher.

It would be curious to know if there were any æsthetic persons present at the Alexandra Palace, among those who enjoyed the novelty of a kid dinner, given by the "British Goat Society" about a year ago (1880). At this dinner— to quote the account then given in the *Daily News*—"the Honorary Secretary confessed to having slaughtered two of his own goats' kids, amid the tears of his children, to satisfy the appetites of the guests, and the statement was heard without eliciting any visible sign of remorse from the company."

We are inclined to think that the æsthetic taste of those who could hear this statement, without showing very visible signs of dissatisfaction, must have been of a somewhat questionable character.

But it is needless to refer to individual instances of bad taste, when all the country is filled with the pollution of wholesale slaughter. Dwellers in London, of superior sensibility, frequently express their disgust at the unsightly streets and buildings which everywhere meet the view, and their pity for the gross tastes and habits of their fellow-townsmen. Yet they raise no protest against the Foreign Cattle Market of Deptford, from which the wants of Londoners are largely supplied; though the deeds which are daily enacted there are such as can hardly commend themselves to an æsthetic mind. At Deptford, as we learn from a lately-published account, there weekly arrive some three thousand bullocks, twenty thousand sheep, and a thousand calves. When they are landed at the entrance, "the creatures, to do them justice, are not often ill-conducted. Stupefied by the voyage, they are generally quiet enough, but sometimes the truth breaks in upon them, and they make a desperate effort for freedom. It is easy to guess what frightens them, for there is a strange scent in the air." Such are the circumstances under which the animals enter these slaughter-houses, all of them, be it remembered, naturally harmless and gentle. They are finally "conducted to the long range of narrow stalls at the rear of the slaughter-houses. The scene is here busy enough, and the celerity with which the work is done sufficiently remarkable—at the one end the fine great beasts go in, at the other emerge great sides of beef, hoofs, hides, and horns. There is much less uproar over the sheep, which are killed and dressed with great celerity."

Pitiable indeed must be the mental and moral condition of those who can read such an account as this without loathing and disgust. And if the mere mention of it is well-nigh intolerable, what is to be said of the system which necessitates the continual enactment of such scenes? Can any thoughtful man, in the face of such horrors, deliberately choose to be a flesh-eater? Must he not rather turn with relief to a vegetarian diet, with which alone can exist that widely sympathetic intellectual gentleness which recognises the rights, not of man only, but of all the animal creation. To repeat the oft-quoted but seldom-appreciated lines of Coleridge—

> "He prayeth best that loveth best
> All things, both great and small:
> For the dear God, who loveth us,
> He made and loveth all."

This brings me to the subject of higher æstheticism, the only true worship of the beautiful, that which does not regard only the perceptions of the senses, but admits the consideration of the moral and the humane. Such a doctrine finds its fullest development in the works of Mr. Ruskin, a teacher whom we Food Reformers, in common with all who strive after a purer life, must revere above all living writers. The superiority of his teaching to that of the æsthetic school in general is due to the fact that he has not thought it necessary to divorce morality from art, but has shown that the consideration of morality is inseparable from true art, as also from true political economy, and indeed from any true science whatever. But alas! *"non omnia possumus omnes;"* and it must be confessed that, on the subject of humanity, Mr. Ruskin's teaching is not quite self-consistent; while his utterances on the subject of Vegetarianism show that he has never really given it his serious attention, though in the last number of *Fors Clavigera*[2] he seems inclined to reconsider the question. Of all great writers Mr. Ruskin is the one from whom the advocates of Food Reform might most reasonably expect at least a word of sympathy and assistance; he is the one who is least able, if he wishes to be self-consistent, to disregard the aspirations of Vegetarianism.

"Without perfect sympathy with the animals around them, no gentleman's education, no Christian education, could be of any possible use." So he said in 1877; and I am not aware that he has ever explained how perfect sympathy with the animals around us can be coexistent with the system of breeding and slaughtering them for food. Again, Rule 5 of Mr. Ruskin's Society of St. George runs as follows: "I will not kill nor hurt any living creature needlessly, nor destroy any beautiful thing, but will strive to save and comfort all gentle life, and guard and perfect all natural beauty upon the earth." These are noble words, and they express the very essence and spirit of the Vegetarian movement; indeed, it is difficult to see how they can be uttered, consistently and conscientiously, by any but Vegetarians. The only loop-hole of escape for the flesh-eater seems to lie in the word *"needlessly,"* and of course the impossibility of Vegetarianism once proved would be a real justification of flesh-eating. It is evident, however, from the May number of *Fors Clavigera*, that Mr. Ruskin is fully aware of the practicability, if not the desirability, of the reformed diet, for he speaks approvingly of Mrs. Nisbet's "very valuable" letter on Vegetarianism to the *Dunfermline Journal*. It is therefore incumbent on the members of St. George's Society to obey the rules of their order by ceasing to uphold the needless, and therefore cruel, institution of the slaughter-house, and by adopting that diet which alone is in harmony with the instincts of morality and good taste.

---

[2] May, 1883.

SOME RESULTS OF FOOD REFORM.

Those who make conscientious trial of a vegetarian diet will find, after two or three years' experience, that they have secured three main advantages. Their health will be better, their household expenses will be less, and they will have the satisfaction of feeling that they are in no way responsible for the cruelties of the slaughter-house. But, in addition to the direct benefits, there are various indirect and incidental results which are worthy of far more serious consideration than they usually receive.

I. First among these, and of most pressing interest at the present day, is the remarkable fact that abstinence from animal food almost invariably brings with it abstinence from all alcoholic drinks. In ninety-nine cases out of a hundred, the Vegetarian will be a total abstainer; not merely because the desire of stimulating drink dies a natural death in the absence of stimulating food, but also because those who have learnt the charm of simplicity in diet are not likely to care for drinks which are unnecessary and expensive. The adoption of a vegetarian diet-system would strike at the root of intemperance among well-to-do people, by the reduction of over-stimulating foods and the promotion of general frugality of living.

Again, on the other hand, if Vegetarian principles were more widely understood and practised, there would be a much larger supply of cheap and wholesome food within the reach of our lower orders; and the chief cause of drunkenness among the poor—their destitution and hunger—might be gradually and surely eradicated. Thus the intemperate habits of the over-fed rich and of the under-fed poor would be checked by one and the same principle of Food Reform. Vegetarianism would teach the rich the great lesson that "Enough is as good as a feast," and also that water is as good a drink as wine; while it would provide the poor with plenty of cheap and nourishing food, and leave them no excuse for having recourse to the pot-house and gin-shop. If the poor could be taught the value of whole-meal bread, oatmeal, and lentils, a greater blow would be dealt at intemperance than by a thousand lectures and addresses.

On these grounds all those who are interested in the temperance movement—and what sane man is not?—should at least consider attentively the arguments advanced in favour of Vegetarianism. More immediate and crying evil is undeniably caused by the use of alcohol than by the use of flesh; and the temperance question is therefore, in one sense, of more urgent importance than that of Food Reform. But in the long run Vegetarianism is vastly more important than teetotalism, inasmuch as the larger question includes the smaller one in itself. If Food Reform be once established Drink Reform will inevitably follow; but as long as flesh-food is largely eaten no lectures on temperance, or Good Templar meetings, or establishment of coffee-houses, or Acts of Parliament, will succeed in extirpating our national vice of drunkenness. The roast beef of old England has done its work, and the natural result has followed.

II. Another habit which is rendered almost impossible by a fleshless diet is that of smoking. A Vegetarian has as little liking for tobacco as for alcohol, and if our diet-system were reformed we should soon cease to prefer tobacco-fumes to pure air. There is no need to enlarge here on the injurious effects of tobacco-smoking; nay, we may even afford to admit for the time that the habit is as innocuous as its votaries assert. Yet when we hear smokers declare that tobacco is a "blessing" to men, because it soothes their mental troubles and enables them to work more contentedly, we cannot but retort that a person who lives a happy and active life, without the use of any narcotic, must be in a far sounder and healthier state than one who needs it. In other words, the use of tobacco is in no case a positive good to men; but at the utmost the lesser of two evils. If we cannot enjoy life and do our duty without inhaling smoke, then by all means let us go at once to the tobacconist's; but at least let us not be silly enough to imagine that other people are less happy because they do not smoke. "A wholesome taste for cleanliness and fresh air," says Ruskin, "is one of the final attainments of humanity. There are not many European gentlemen, even in the highest classes who have a pure and right love of fresh air. They would put the filth of tobacco even into the first breeze of a May morning." Vegetarianism may or may not be the foolish theory that some shrewd people would have it appear; but it certainly has the practical advantage of effectually abolishing any desire for tobacco-smoke.

III. But besides these definite results, the Vegetarian will find himself a great gainer in what I may call general simplicity, or good taste in diet. I do not, of course, mean to assert that this is a virtue special to Vegetarians, to which no flesh-eater can attain; but merely that the Vegetarian, *cæteris paribus*, is more likely to be wise and thoughtful about his diet than a flesh-eater. For there is "good taste" in eating and drinking, as in all other things, and that style of diet is obviously in best taste which keeps the body in most equable health, neither pampering it by over-feeding nor weakening by excessive abstinence. This golden mean between gluttony on the one side and asceticism on the other, would be more widely attained if the use of flesh-food were discontinued. For the Vegetarian, who understands the importance of the question of diet, is, as a rule, less likely to eat too much than those who never consider the nature of their food; and he will be wiser not only in the quantity but also in the quality of what he eats. Among Vegetarians there will be no such vulgar perversions of taste as among those who affect to find a delicacy in venison and game when it is "high," or in cheese when it is "ripe;" or, still worse, in the grosser inventions of the gourmand, where cruelty as well as vulgarity has done its work; in the white veal and crimped cod, and other dishes that shall be here unmentioned. Let flesh-eaters relish these their delights; but as the food of the Vegetarian will be moderate in quantity, so in quality it will be fresh and simple and pure.

But moderation is also far removed from asceticism, which is merely the reaction against gross feeding, and would never have come into existence under a simple and natural system of living. Under a Vegetarian régime there will be no asceticism, which has been the weakness—I will not say the fault—of many a high and noble nature, and cannot be in itself good or desirable. Those who weaken the body by excessive privations must weaken the mind also, and will consequently be less able to do good in the world than those who practise a wise and unvarying moderation.

And lastly, it may be well to point out *why* a Vegetarian diet, which would thus establish temperance without austerity, and liberality without extravagance, is, from an intellectual point of view, to be regarded as of such extreme importance. And here I cannot resist the desire of quoting a remarkable passage from a pamphlet published by the Vegetarian Society[3]—

---

[3] "Simplicity of Tastes," by the Rev. C. H. Collyns.

"Can you imagine a gross feeder on turtle-soup or venison, high game, and rotten cheese, a self-indulgent drinker, being a man of bright, pure, simple tastes and instincts? Would you go to such a man and expect him to catch the ethereal beauties of some of Shelley's choicer pieces? . . . You would not; you would feel, and justly, that such perceptions were too fine, too delicate for him: that the animal was too strong in him; the mind, the spirit, too little, too weak, too puny for such higher thoughts as these." Grossness of diet is indeed a fertile cause of dulness and dejection of mind, and therefore we find that most great men have been abstemious in their way of living, and especially so when occupied on any great work. The complaint of Sir Andrew Aguecheek in *Twelfth Night*—"I am a great eater of beef, and I believe that does harm to my wit"—is only one instance of many recognitions of a remarkable psychological fact. Perhaps the most comprehensive reason ever urged against the use of flesh-food is to be found in the saying attributed, I know not on what authority, to Lamartine, that "he had no right to make himself stupider than God made him."

In some cases it would be a difficult task to effect this. But alas! is it not a task that is daily being attempted, with more or less success, in the houses of many of our flesh-eating friends who "keep a good table?"

MEDICAL MEN AND FOOD REFORM.

The commonest obstacle to Food Reform, as indeed to every other Reform, is prejudice. The popular belief that flesh-food is the best diet for mankind is so deeply rooted in the minds of every class of Englishmen, from highest to lowest, that we cannot reasonably hope to eradicate it all at once. We can only look for the gradual conversion of the most intellectual classes, and the consequent spread of wiser dietetic views to the rest of the community. In the meantime it is well worth our while to consider one remarkable fact often urged against us by our adversaries, that among special classes or professions the one which is most strongly opposed to Vegetarianism is that of medical men. There are, of course, many notable exceptions.[4] We, too, can appeal to illustrious names in support of our arguments; but it is nevertheless undeniable that nearly all ordinary physicians entirely condemn the principles of Food Reform, and believe animal food to be most desirable, if not absolutely necessary, for good health.

How are we Vegetarians to explain this fact? The influence of medical men, both on public and private opinion, is unquestionably very great, and at present nearly the whole weight of this influence is thrown into the scale against us. What answer are we to make to the question, so often asked— "Why are so few doctors Vegetarians?"

Some Food Reformers do not scruple to impute dishonest motives to the medical profession, and hint that doctors disparage Food Reform because they would find their occupation gone or greatly limited, if a more natural and simple diet-system were generally adopted. Such imputation seems to me to be singularly unfortunate, being not only foolish in itself (for the introduction of Vegetarianism, being necessarily very gradual, would injure no class interests whatever), but also most damaging to the cause of Food Reform, which can ill afford to substitute insinuation for argument. We ought rather

---

[4] *Vide* Sir Henry Thompson's article on Food—*Nineteenth Century*, June and July, 1879, and May, 1885.

candidly to admit that the opinion of medical men is hostile to Food Reform, and to attempt to discover the reason of an antagonism which we must necessarily deplore.

Vegetarians are generally well able to hold their own in argument against flesh-eaters, when the diet question is discussed in ordinary conversation. But there is certainly something a trifle embarrassing in the position of a Food Reformer who, being as ignorant as most people of the details of physiology, may chance to find himself landed in unequal controversy with a medical man full of technical knowledge and scientific precision. Can he venture to adhere to his own unprofessional opinions, in spite of the distinct assurance of his learned antagonist that he has specially studied this subject and satisfied himself beyond a doubt that flesh-food is necessary for mankind? Can he doggedly maintain that he lives in the best of health without meat, in opposition to one who blandly but firmly assures him (with perfect knowledge of his internal construction), that he is entirely mistaken? In short, can he rely on his own native common-sense, when it is apparently in conflict with the professional knowledge of a specialist?

I think that he can. For it should be observed that "the great food question," as it has been truly called, is not merely one of the many medical subjects which may be successfully studied and systematised by chemists and doctors, still less a mere scientific fact which can be demonstrated with mathematical precision, but a matter of far wider import, a many-sided problem which can only be solved by a delicate appreciation of the tastes, feelings, and practical experience of mankind. I believe that a physician, in his capacity of physician, is no better qualified than any ordinary person to decide such a question.

Indeed, all such questions must be decided finally by natural instinct and experience, rather than by technical knowledge; by innate wisdom rather than by acquired learning. This fact is seen in every branch of art and science, from the humblest to the highest. A bootmaker is the best possible authority on the particular subject of bootmaking, but it would not be wise to consult him on the general study of the human foot and the style of covering most suitable thereto. A tailor is undeniably a valuable adviser about coats and trousers, but it would be a sign of ill-placed confidence if one blindly accepted his opinion on the wider question of appropriate national costumes. So, too, in intellectual matters. One would scarcely look to a schoolmaster who has devoted a lifetime to one particular system for an unprejudiced opinion on the general question of education; or to a sectarian preacher for liberal views on theology. In fact, it seems as if all special professions have to some extent a narrowing influence on the mind, which in ordinary cases prevents specialists forming an unbiassed judgment on any question which extends beyond the precise limits of their actual professional practice. This principle is recognised in many of our institutions. The jurymen, for instance, who decide lawsuits; the governing bodies who rule our public schools; even the ministers chosen to superintend the various departments of our government, are not trained officials whose minds have long been moulded in the professional groove, but private individuals who may bring to their duties the advantage of clear unprejudiced judgment and sound common-sense. Of course it is not to be denied that it would be still better if professional knowledge could always go hand in hand, as it sometimes does, with perfect mental impartiality; but as this is unfortunately seldom the case we are bound to choose the lesser of two evils. We prefer, in matters of wide interest, to trust to our private judgment and experience, rather than to any professional advice; because we find that professional men, being entirely committed to one line of thought, are usually more liable to prejudice than private individuals.

A good example of the fallibility of the medical profession may be seen in the history of the temperance question. Not many years ago a vast majority of medical men unhesitatingly affirmed, on scientific grounds, that the use of alcoholic drinks is beneficial and even necessary, and much ridicule was lavished on those who, relying upon personal taste and practical experience, took the contrary view. Now the laugh is on the other side, and the immense progress of the temperance movement has proved beyond doubt that our doctors were wrong. But if our medical advisers, who professed to be able to tell us what to drink, have erred so egregiously in the question of liquor, is it so incredible that they are making a similar mistake in the question of food?

The truth is that medical men are very far from being infallible, either in their individual opinion or collective judgment. Prejudice often affects classes as strongly as individuals, and the class of which I am speaking is certainly no exception to the rule. Trained in a special school of medicine, with many immemorial and therefore unquestioned traditions as to the relative utility of various kinds of food and drink, what wonder if medical men are disturbed and irritated by the suggestion that their whole diet-system is based on an insecure foundation? And this is precisely what Food Reformers assert, when they advocate the disuse of all stimulants in food as well as in drink, and condemn flesh-meat no less than alcohol.

It is therefore no marvel that Food Reform has hitherto received but little encouragement from the medical profession. A system of plain food and natural simplicity of life is not likely to find favour with those who conscientiously believe that they can make us for the present a moderately healthy and happy nation by feeding us with butchers' meat and vaccinating us against our will; while they turn a wistful eye to vivisection, in the hope of a shower of yet more beneficent discoveries in the future.

On the other hand, we Vegetarians need not be the least alarmed or disconcerted by finding the medical profession arrayed in arms against us. Their intentions are beyond doubt excellent; but, like other good people, they require time to take in new ideas. We must not wonder if they show signs of some vexation, and do all they can (which is a good deal) to retard the cause of Food Reform, for it is undoubtedly irritating to them to find the rude test of practical experience applied to the delicate theories of medical science. When doctors have declared that their patients cannot live without meat, how annoying and perplexing it must be to see them thriving on a vegetarian diet! We can at least comfort ourselves with the recollection that on other questions medical men have repeatedly shifted their ground, when proved by time to be hopelessly in error; from which we may venture to predict that in like manner they will eventually change their opinion even on the question of diet.

SIR HENRY THOMPSON ON "DIET."

Sir Henry Thompson's article on "Diet," published in the May number of the *Nineteenth Century*, 1885, has probably given considerably more satisfaction to Food Reformers than to members of the medical profession. For, though Sir Henry Thompson takes especial care to disavow the slightest sympathy with what is known as the "Vegetarian" movement, and though his *esprit de corps* leads him to make a sharp attack on the Vegetarian Society, yet his article is practically an admission of what the Vegetarians have been preaching for the last ten or twenty years—viz., that flesh-food is unnecessary in a temperate climate. This admission is, of course, most valuable to Food Reformers, as coming from one of the most distinguished members of a profession which is still hostile, in the main, to the spread of the reformed diet; and we can therefore pardon Sir Henry Thompson for his somewhat bitter remarks about Vegetarianism as a dietary system, more especially as they are entirely irrelevant to the real subject of discussion.

"An exclusive or sectarian spirit," he says, "always creeps in sooner or later wherever an 'ism' of any kind leads the way." This may conceivably be a valid objection to the whole system of forming societies in order to propagate any particular doctrine; but it certainly has no special applicability to the Vegetarian movement; and it would not be difficult to show that this "exclusive or sectarian spirit" has manifested itself quite as strongly in the medical profession as in any recently-formed society. But, passing this over, I must protest against Sir Henry Thompson's extraordinary assertion that, in calling themselves "Vegetarians," Food Reformers, who for the most part use eggs and milk, have deliberately sacrificed accuracy of expression, in order to gain the small distinction of a party name. It is quite true that most—not all— Food Reformers admit into their diet such animal food as milk, butter, cheese, and eggs, and, therefore, the term "Vegetarian,' as applied to these, is not an accurate one; but it is quite a mistake to imagine that this misleading title is coveted or purposely retained by the Vegetarians themselves. On the contrary, the desirability of finding a more suitable name has again and again been discussed in the pages of the *Dietetic Reformer*; and there has been no attempt whatever on the part of the Vegetarian Society, or its members, to claim the merit of a purely vegetable diet. But the fact is, that the word "Vegetarian," in its general application to those who abstain from flesh, has long become too firmly fixed in the language to admit of any sudden limitation or restriction. It is the most difficult thing in the world to alter a word which has once become nationalised in a particular sense; and the reason why Food Reformers are still called "Vegetarians" is simply that nobody has yet been able to suggest any title which would have the least chance of ousting the more popular term. "I feel sure," says Sir Henry Thompson, "that my friends 'the Vegetarians,' living on a mixed diet, will see the necessity of seeking a more appropriate designation to distinguish them; if not, we must endeavour to invent one for them." If Sir Henry Thompson will make this endeavour, all Vegetarians will be sincerely grateful to him; at present the only alternative title seems to be the word "Akreophagist," which is hardly likely to take permanent root in the English language.

But this attack on Vegetarians, for the use of a title which they have long been vainly trying to get rid of, is surely made by Sir Henry Thompson rather as a diversion than as a serious part of his article. It is thrown out as a sop to Cerberus, who, in the form of the medical profession, might otherwise be grievously chagrined at this unexpected corroboration of the ignorant and unprofessional assertions of Food Reformers. When medical men have been telling their patients, with more and more persistence, that it is impossible to live healthily without using flesh-food, it is, of course, very annoying and irritating to find the most eminent of English surgeons admitting precisely the contrary. To cover their retreat, and mitigate their possible resentment, Sir Henry Thompson mercifully determined to make this timely diversion by abusing the Vegetarians roundly, while thoroughly endorsing the essence of their teaching. Our medical friends are welcome to whatever cold comfort they can derive from Sir Henry Thompson's dislike of Vegetarian propagandists and Vegetarianism as a system; but, in the meantime, we Vegetarians, or Food Reformers, or Akreophagists, or whatever it may please the British public to call us, are quite clear on this one point. It is the substance that we care for, and not the shadow. We have long asserted that flesh-food is not, as the doctors would have had us believe, a necessary part of our English diet system; and this, our chief contention, is now explicitly admitted by Sir Henry Thompson. "It is a vulgar error," he says, "to regard meat in any form as necessary to life." Precisely so; that has been the sum and substance of our teaching during the last quarter of a century, in spite of every sort of denial, ridicule, and misrepresentation; and now that medical men are beginning to find they were after all in the wrong, they ingeniously attempt to cover their own confusion by raising a perfectly irrelevant cuckoo-cry about the title of their opponents. Let them call us anything they will—the mere name is quite immaterial to *us*;—but at least let them have the candour to admit that we were right, and they were wrong, as regards the necessity of the slaughter-house.

However, as Sir Henry Thompson has thought fit to challenge our position on this question of the use of eggs and dairy produce, it may be well to consider it more fully. It is quite a mistake to suppose, as he seems to imply, that Food Reformers use eggs and milk very largely as a substitute for flesh; on the contrary, I believe that most of us use them sparingly and in moderation, believing, as Sir Henry Thompson himself remarks, that "for us who have long ago achieved our full growth, and can thrive on solid fare, milk is altogether superfluous and mostly mischievous as a drink." Milk, as it has been well said, is "an excellent thing—for calves;" and Food Reformers, for the most part, being well aware of this, are careful *not* to use dairy produce in the quantity mentioned by Sir Henry Thompson. But why, it may be asked, do they not renounce eggs and milk altogether, and thus establish an unequivocal claim to the title of Vegetarian? To this it must be answered that the immediate object which Food Reformers aim at is not so much the disuse of animal substances in general, as the abolition of flesh-meat in particular; and that, if they can drive their opponents to make the very important admission that actual flesh-food is unnecessary, they can afford to smile at the trivial retort that animal substance is still used in eggs and milk. It is not the mere name of *"animal"* food they are afraid of, but they consider the use of butcher's meat at once unpleasant and degrading, though, as such strong objections cannot be urged against dairy produce, many who abstain from beef and mutton continue to use eggs, milk, cheese, and butter. There is, of course, the additional reason that it is hard all at once to make the complete change to a strictly vegetarian diet, and many Food Reformers are glad to use eggs and milk as being at present cheap and plentiful, and as affording a *modus vivendi* to those who might otherwise be entirely cut off by dietetic differences from the society of their friends, though, at the same time, they are well aware that even dairy produce is quite unnecessary and superfluous, and will doubtlessly be dispensed with altogether under a more natural system of diet. In the meantime, however, one step is sufficient. Let us first recognise the fact that the institution of the slaughter-house, with all its attendant horrors, is one that might easily be abolished; that point gained, the question of the total disuse of all animal products is one that will easily be decided hereafter. What I wish to insist on is that it is not "animal" food which we Food Reformers primarily abjure, but nasty food, expensive food, and unwholesome food. It is, therefore, absurd to twit us with the use of eggs and milk, because we do not eat fowls and beef. And the climax of absurdity is reached when Sir Henry Thompson gravely points out to us that the infant who thrives on mother's milk is not subsisting on vegetarian diet! Talk of "equivocal terms, evasion,— in short, untruthfulness!'" Was there ever such evasion of the real issue as this? It would be equally logical and scientific to argue that a cow must be classed among the *carnivora*, because a calf drinks milk.

Another point on which Sir Henry Thompson again and again insists in his paper on "Diet" is that it is unwise to limit in any way the choice of foods. "The great practical rule of life," he says, "in regard to human diet will not be found in enforcing limitation of the sources of food which nature has abundantly provided." I may here remark in passing that Sir Henry Thompson's reference to the Esquimaux, as an instance of a people to whom a vegetarian diet would be impossible, is not of much practical value to English readers in the elucidation of this food question; for we desire to know what diet system is appropriate to the inhabitants of the temperate zones, and not those of the arctic circle. However, as far as the purely *physical* aspect of the food question is concerned, Food Reformers may be quite content to agree to Sir Henry Thompson's opinion that we ought not "to limit man's liberty to select his food and drink." Everybody must choose for himself on this most important question, for "no man," as Sir Henry Thompson wisely remarks, "can tell another what he can or ought to eat without knowing what are the habits of life and work—mental and bodily—of the person to be advised." Still, it does not constitute a very serious or insidious attack on individual liberty to point out, as the Vegetarian Society does, what advantages have been found in a particular line of diet by a large number of people. There is nothing dogmatic or sectarian in teaching of this kind; indeed, it is adopted by Sir Henry Thompson himself in this same article, when he speaks of the question of alcohol. "It is rare now," he says, "to find any one, well acquainted with human physiology, and capable of observing and appreciating the ordinary wants and usages of life around him, who does not believe that, with few exceptions, men and women are healthier and stronger physically, intellectually, and morally—without such drinks than with them." Substitute the word *food* for *drink*, and you have an exact exposition of the Vegetarian doctrine.

But I must now return to our main position. We have it emphatically stated, on the authority of Sir Henry Thompson, that in a temperate climate, such as that in which we live, flesh-food is not necessary.[5] He qualifies this admission by repeatedly stating that he does not wish to dispense with it altogether in its proper place and time; but though he hints that flesh-food may at times be "desirable, and even essential to life," he nowhere gives any clear indication of when this necessity may arise. But now come in other aspects of the case which are wholly ignored by Sir Henry Thompson in his purely professional treatment of it. He has given us an entirely medical and scientific view of this subject of diet, and the upshot of what he says is this: "Flesh-food is quite unnecessary in the large majority of cases, but you had better eat a little now and then for fear you should become sectarian and narrow-minded, and thus cause the exclusion of any of the recognised sources of food." *Cæteris paribus*, this statement of the case is most unobjectionable and satisfactory; but, unfortunately for Sir Henry Thompson's conclusions, there are various other considerations which (however uninteresting to medical men) are of the greatest possible importance to the unprofessional mind. In the choice of our food we have not only to ask our doctors what are the latest conclusions of scientific inquiry; but we have also to consider what

---

[5] Sir Henry Thompson makes a possible exception in the case of hard-working out-door labourers; but this seems hardly justified by experience, as the labouring classes are precisely those who successfully perform a maximum of labour with a minimum of flesh-food. Contrast Dr. W. B. Carpenter's remark: "We freely concede to the advocates of Vegetarianism that, as regards the endurance of *physical* labour, there is ample proof of the capacity of their diet to afford the requisite sustenance."

are the promptings of economy, humanity, and good taste. All this is naïvely passed over by Sir Henry Thompson; but I hardly think the question will be allowed to rest in the position where he seems to wish to leave it. "Unnecessary, but sometimes desirable," is hardly the last word to be said on the subject of butchers' meat. Unnecessary it certainly is. But is it desirable? There is a good deal to be said on that point, too!

The question of *economy* in diet is just hinted at, and no more, in Sir Henry Thompson's article. Yet surely, at the present time, when a social crisis seems to be impending at no distant date, owing to the terrible destitution of the lower classes, it is a question worthy of the most earnest consideration of every thoughtful man. Every housekeeper knows to her cost that butcher's bills form the most serious item of the weekly account, and the sum total spent by the nation on this form of food is something enormous. On the other hand, it is equally indisputable that there are many cheap kinds of vegetable food which are as nutritive or *more* nutritive than flesh meat; and it has repeatedly been shown that every shilling spent on beef or mutton might have purchased five or six times the amount of nutriment if expended on peas, beans, lentils, wholemeal bread, or oatmeal. Mr. Hoyle has calculated that, if every family in the kingdom were to reduce its consumption of butcher's meat by one pound's weight only, there would be an annual saving of at least ten millions of money. Statistics are proverbially an unsatisfactory method of argument; but, even at the lowest computation, it cannot be denied that our food supply would be enormously increased if the use of flesh meat were entirely discontinued.[6] Nor would this direct saving be by any means the only benefit resulting from the change. If the towns renounced flesh eating, it would no longer be worth a landlord's while to keep arable land in pasture, and the result

---

[6] It is worth remarking that, though Sir Henry Thompson scarcely mentions the question of economy in his latest article on "Diet," he dealt rather more fully with it in the June number of the *Nineteenth Century* for 1879. He there wrote: "These things being so, a consideration of no small concern arises in relation to the economical management of the national resources. For it is a fair computation that every acre of land devoted to the production of meat is capable of becoming the source of three or four times the amount of produce of equivalent value of food, if devoted to the production of grain. In other words, a given area of land cropped with cereals and legumes will support a population more than three times as numerous as that which can be sustained on the same land devoted to the growth of cattle." Of late Sir Henry Thompson seems to have overlooked this very important consideration.

would be an immense development of rustic industry; for, instead of a few men tending oxen, there would be large numbers employed in growing crops. Thus the stream of migration from country to town, which is at present so much deplored by all who are interested in the welfare of the poor, would be checked and turned backwards to the country. From whatever point of view we regard this question—the interest of the individual, or the interest of the community—it appears to be equally undeniable that an immense saving may be effected by the substitution of vegetable for animal food; and, therefore, this question of economy cannot possibly be overlooked by anyone who wishes to arrive at a sound and trustworthy conclusion as regards the choice of diet. Nothing can be more emphatic than the opinion of Dr. B. W. Richardson (and it would be difficult to name a more competent authority) on this necessity for thrift. "We have also to learn," he says, "as a first truth, that the oftener we go to the vegetable world for our food the oftener we go to the first, and, therefore, to the *cheapest*, source of supply. The commonly accepted notion that, when we eat animal flesh, we are eating food at its prime source, cannot be too speedily dissipated, or too speedily replaced by the knowledge that there is no primitive form of food—albuminous, starchy, osseous—in the animal world itself; and that all the processes of catching an inferior animal, of breeding it, rearing it, keeping it, killing it, dressing it, and selling it, mean no more and no less than *entirely additional expenditure* throughout for bringing into what we have been taught to consider an acceptable form of food the veritable food which the animal itself found, without any such preparation, in the vegetable world." This being so, let us recur to the point to which Sir Henry Thompson brought us. If flesh-food be, as he admits, entirely unnecessary, will not this additional consideration of economy turn the balance when we make our choice of diet? Will a nation whose food supply is becoming a matter of more and more anxiety persist in spending six times as much money as it is obliged to spend, in order that it may not interfere with "the present generally recognised sources and varieties of food?" Are we to renounce the full economic advantages of a vegetarian diet system, because we are reminded that an infant is nourished on milk and Esquimaux on blubber?

Then, again, there is the plea of *humanity*—unmentioned throughout Sir Henry Thompson's article. If the purse is worthy of consideration in the settlement of this question, the heart can hardly be disregarded. And in spite of all the sneers that are often levelled at humanitarians and "sentimentalists," I believe that there is a very real and very strong feeling among most people about this institution of the slaughter-house, though if ever they manifest any qualm of an awakening conscience they are speedily reassured by the family physician, who informs them that he has specially studied these matters, and that it is madness to attempt to live without butcher's meat. Well, indeed, would it be if all kindly people who say a "grace" over their food would think of the history of such a meal! If they would reflect on the agony of terror endured by imported cattle during the journey by sea or land; the disease too often engendered by the filth and misery of the voyage; the thirst, the hunger, the despair, and, finally, the horrors of the slaughter-house; and, then, if they would recollect Sir Henry Thompson's words, "It is a vulgar error to regard meat in any form as necessary to life," I fancy they would hardly care to continue their flesh-eating habits, merely in order to avoid adopting an "ism," or limiting the present varieties of food."

We started with the admission that everybody must consult his own experience and taste in the matter of food, and I have now stated what seem to me to be the chief considerations worthy of notice in this choice of diet. On the one hand, we have Sir Henry Thompson's assertion that flesh meat, though confessedly unnecessary, may at times, and in smaller measure, be desirable; on the other hand, we have to weigh well the fact (unnoticed by Sir Henry Thompson) that flesh-food is five or six times as expensive as vegetable substance; that the institution of the slaughter-house entails cruel sufferings on millions upon millions of innocent animals; and that our tables are thereby supplied with a far less appetising and agreeable form of food than that which good taste would bid us desire. Surely, under these conditions of choice, "Vegetarianism," "Food Reform," "Akreophagy"—whatever we like to call it—is worthy of a far more earnest trial than even the most advanced member of the medical profession seems at present willing to allow it.

ON CERTAIN FALLACIES.

The object of this paper is to meet some of the stock arguments that are most commonly advanced by the opponents of Food Reform, and to prove in each case that for those who are once convinced of the desirability of a vegetarian diet, there is no insuperable difficulty in carrying their wishes into practical effect. In nine cases out of ten it will be found that these objections to Vegetarianism are based on no solid and rational grounds, but rather on certain prejudices which have taken deep root in the British mind, and are in one form or another continually reappearing. I am aware that in refuting these time-honoured fallacies, I am only going over ground which has already been repeatedly traversed. But as long as our opponents persist in advancing the same arguments, we Vegetarians may be pardoned for reproducing the same replies.

1. "*The Teeth.*" One of the first objections by which flesh-eaters attempt to throw discredit on Food Reform, is the statement that the impossibility of a vegetarian diet is demonstrated by the formation of the teeth and other structural evidence. "Comparative anatomy," they say, "shows distinctly that the human teeth and intestines are constructed with a view to the digestion of flesh, and not of vegetables." The answer to this very fallacious assertion is simply a denial *in toto*. Flesh-eaters are utterly mistaken in the assertion they rashly make, and if they will examine their authorities more carefully, they will discover that the comparative anatomy to which they appeal establishes beyond any doubt the *frugivorous*, not carnivorous, origin of man. "The natural food of man," says Cuvier, "judging from his structure, appears to consist principally of the fruits, roots, and other succulent parts of vegetables" This opinion is corroborated by that of Linnæus, M. Gassendi, Ray, Professor Owen, Professor Lawrence, and a host of other authorities; but even without any scientific testimony, the fact that the apes, who are nearest akin to us in the animal world, are frugivorous, is a somewhat strong indication that flesh is not the natural food of mankind.

2. Our opponents next take refuge in the very specious fallacy that "*Vegetarianism is impossible in cold climates.*" We are reminded that our climate is not a tropical one; that Vegetarianism may be all very well in warm and sunny regions, but that in this land of cold and mist "the roast beef of old England" alone can cheer and support us. We reply that actual experience shows this to be erroneous. Those who have conscientiously made a trial of vegetarian diet have not found climatic influences the smallest obstacle in their path. An English winter is undoubtedly depressing, but it is not more so because one's food is pure.

3. The baffled advocate of flesh-eating now changes his ground, and adopts a high moral tone, pointing out at the same time some incidental difficulties and drawbacks of Food Reform. "*Vegetarianism involves too much thinking about one's food.*" Hard-working men often seem to think there is a sort of merit in "not caring what one eats." This is a fallacy; for though it is meritorious to be able to content oneself with plain fare, yet mere indifference about one's food can only arise from stupidity or thoughtlessness, since the welfare of mind involves excessive thinking about one's food? A change of diet undoubtedly necessitates some temporary consideration; new recipes have to be found, and substitutes for "meat" must be tried; but this is not an inherent or perpetual characteristic of a vegetarian régime, which, when once fairly started, is far simpler and less troublesome than the system of flesh-eating. If Vegetarianism had existed as a national custom for some centuries, and flesh-food were now being introduced as a novelty, precisely the same objection might be urged on the other side; it would then be the flesh-eater who would be obliged to hunt out recipes and "think about his food." And he would have a much less pleasant subject to think about.

4. "*Vegetarianism is a mere crotchet.*" This is a statement which often does much injury to the cause of Food Reform, by representing it as a fanciful whim, amiable enough and praise-worthy in intention, but undeserving of the consideration of practical men. When there is so much real work to be done in this world, it is childish—so argues the earnest and philanthropic flesh-eater—to waste time on theories which are the mere dreams of humanitarian sentimentalists and fanatical crotchet-mongers. This is an argument which, in the mouth of an unscrupulous opponent, is always sure of a considerable amount of success; for there is no charge of which Englishmen stand in such

mortal and unreasoning terror as the very vague accusation of "sentimentalism." Men who are naturally gentle and kind-hearted, will obstinately close their ears to anything which can expose them to the least suspicion of "sentiment," and will sanction any cruelty rather than run the risk of being ridiculed as "humanitarians." Again, there is a natural disinclination among honest and hard-working men to attend to any new doctrines or speculations which may distract their thoughts from the leading object of their lives, and this disinclination is strengthened tenfold when they are told that the theories in question are visionary and unpractical. Now this is exactly what is constantly being asserted by the opponents of all reforms, not least of Food Reform. Yet, how can Vegetarianism be truthfully described as a mere craze and oddity? It can hardly be denied that it is practicable; for it is seen to be practised by many who owe to it increased health and happiness. Its indubitable economy cannot wisely be disregarded in a country where poverty is as prevalent as in ours. If we are not blinded by prejudice and custom, we should see that the most truly practical man is he who can live most simply, healthily, and contentedly; while the term "crotchet-monger" is to none more fitly applicable than to him who fondly imagines that he cannot live a useful life without costly and unnecessary food. But, alas! this is one of the commonest of all fallacies, to make ourselves believe that those people are "unpractical" who advocate a course of life which we ourselves do not wish to practise.

5. "*We ought to eat meat for the sake of others.*" Selfishness is the next crime with which the Vegetarian is charged. His relatives are anxious about him, for he is delicate by nature, and the doctor has been heard to mutter words of ominous import; the neighbours are beginning to talk; the servants, too, are puzzled and annoyed; the cook grumbles at having to prepare new dishes, and the butcher's tenderest feelings are shocked and violated. Would it not be far nobler and more unselfish on the part of the author of all this trouble, if he would set aside his own personal feelings, and eat meat for the sake of others? This, which may be termed "the family fallacy," is of much the same nature as the last; the only difference being that there it was the fear of sentimentalism, here it is the fear of selfishness that is used as a powerful lever to warp the reasoning powers of the unwary. The fallacy lies in representing Vegetarianism as a mere idle whim and personal predilection, such as it would

indeed be selfish to practise, where it caused trouble or anxiety to others. But all true Food Reformers know that it is much more than this: a man who has once understood the full meaning and value of Food Reform cannot return to a flesh-diet, for any motive. however specious, without wronging and ruining the whole spirit of his life. In a case where one feels as strongly as this, it is no question of selfishness or unselfishness; it is a sheer absurdity for a man to give up what he feels to be true and right. No person in the world is justified in demanding such a sacrifice as this, and no Vegetarian is justified in granting it if demanded.

6. *"What should we do without leather?"* is perhaps the commonest of a host of questions of a similar kind, the object of which is to show to what desperate straits civilised men would be reduced, if they were deprived of the use of animal substances. Jocose flesh-eaters take a malicious delight in pointing out and enumerating to Vegetarians the many animal substances now in common use, and in taunting them with inconsistency in using them. The consistent Food Reformer, they say, must abjure boots and leather in all its forms; he must not even be drawn by a vehicle where the harness is of leather. His books must not be bound in calf; seal-skin and all furs must be banished from his household. Bone, too, must be prohibited; and he must bethink him of some substitute even for soap and candles. All this is amusing enough, but the answer to it is of the simplest and most conclusive kind. The difficulties mentioned are only temporary and incidental, and are merely owing to the fact that the abundance of animal substance from the carcases of slaughtered beasts has naturally been used to supply our wants, to the exclusion of other material. When once the supply of carcases began to diminish, invention would soon be busy, and the wants of man would be equally well supplied from other sources. This process would, of course, be a gradual one, keeping pace exactly with the gradual change from a diet of animal to vegetable food: at no period would there be the smallest confusion or inconvenience to anybody. In the meantime, Vegetarians need not seriously trouble themselves with the foolish charge of "inconsistency." They use leather, etc., now, not from any personal preference for such substances, but because, owing to the unpleasant dietetic habits of other people, it so happens that they can at present get nothing else. It is important, however, for Food Reformers to feel sure that the adoption of their principles would cause

no real and permanent deficiencies in the appliances of civilised life; and on this point I think they may feel easy. We hear of many trivial and hardly serious objections, but I do not think any really necessary or important animal production can be mentioned for which as good a substitute could not easily be supplied from the vegetable or mineral kingdom. It may afford some pleasant mental exercise to our carnivorous friends to tax their ingenuity on this point.

7. And now we come to two of the most amusing and characteristic arguments of our opponents. Finding that direct attacks on Vegetarianism are by no means unanswerable, and that the difficulties of that system are not so insuperable as has been fondly supposed, they have recourse to what may be considered a most ingenious after-thought. They are suddenly filled with profound concern for the true interests of the animals themselves! *"What would become of the animals?"* is a question to which these humane and unselfish disputants invite our serious attention. If they were not killed for food, would they not soon run wild in great numbers, and be reduced to a grievous state through famine and bodily ill-condition? Would they not lie dying in great numbers by a slow and painful death, instead of being quickly and mercifully despatched by the hands of the butcher?

It is almost incredible that any reasoning person should ask such questions as these; yet the fact that they *are* repeatedly asked must be my excuse for spending a few moments in answering them. Some persons are unaware, or affect to be unaware, that even under the present system the increase of domestic animals is not left free and unrestricted; that the cook makes known her demands to the butcher, the butcher in his turn applies to the cattle-breeder, and animals are bred and supplied precisely in proportion to this demand. If Vegetarianism ever became general, only such animals would be bred, and only in such limited numbers as would then be required for the service of men; as, for instance, sheep for their wool, and horses for their value as beasts of burden. This change would, of course, be a gradual one: the demand for other cattle would not cease suddenly, nor would cattle-breeders be ruined by finding their occupation suddenly gone. Nor need we fear that any animals would eventually be left unprovided for on our hands; for there would undoubtedly be some loyal and conservative flesh-eaters, who, faithful to the end, would perform the useful task of eating up any otherwise superfluous oxen and swine. Horses are not at present usually killed for the sake of their flesh; yet it is not found that they run wild in great numbers, or lie dying about our fields. Donkeys are not used for human food; yet it is, proverbially, a rare thing to see a dead donkey. So, too, would it be under a Vegetarian régime. Animals would be bred only in such numbers as were actually required. When they were worn out by old age or disease, they would, if incurable, be mercifully killed and buried.

8. "Ah," says some more profound and metaphysical flesh-eater, "but observe that in thus diminishing the number of animals that are born into the world, you are also diminishing the sum of animal happiness. At present a large number of animals live a happy life, and die a speedy death, and the balance of pleasure must be surely in their favour. *It is better for the animals themselves to live and to be killed, than not to live at all.*"

Such reasoning, if accepted as a justification of flesh-eating, must also justify vivisection or any torture whatever. A vivisector who breeds rabbits for that purpose, might argue that it is better for the rabbits to live a year and be tortured an hour than not to live at all. The humane flesh-eater may be shocked, but if he will examine the argument he will find it precisely identical with his own. This may lead us to suspect the validity of such reasoning, yet it is so frequently advanced by persons of considerable intelligence and education that it deserves to be carefully examined and refuted. Its fallacy arises from a confusion of ideas about "life," as compared with previous existence or non-existence.

Now, animals either exist or do not exist before the commencement of "life." If they do exist, this ante-natal condition may, for all we know, be a happier state than "life," and it is therefore absurd to assert that we do animals a kindness in breeding them. On the other hand, if we assume, as seems most probable, that they do *not* exist before birth, how can the transition from non-existence to existence be shown to be an advantage? That which is non-existent is alike beyond the reach of pleasure or pain, and the terms "good" "bad," "better," "worse," can only apply to that which is already existent. Of the non-existent we can predicate just this—*nothing*. To say, therefore, that we have done a kindness to our born flocks in giving them life, is as sheer and utter nonsense as to say that we have done an *un*kindness to our *un*born flocks, in not making special arrangements for their birth! Or, in other words, a man brings more happiness into the world, in exact proportion as he eats more flesh-meat and enlarges the trade of the butcher and cattle-breeder. If we all resolve to eat twice as much mutton, there will be twice as many sheep, and the beneficent flesh-eater will observe with complacent self-satisfaction twice as much frisking happiness among the lambs in spring-time!

The fact is that the duty of kindness and gentleness to the lower animals begins only at the time of their birth and ends only at their death, nor can it be evaded by any references to ante-natal existence or non-existence. Such devices are only an after-thought by which flesh-eaters try to escape the responsibility of their own acts. It may or may not be better for mankind, that animals should be bred and slaughtered for food: it certainly is not better for the animals themselves.

9. Next we come to what is sometimes described as the great justification of flesh-eating, the argument drawn from nature. Flesh-eating, it is said, cannot be immoral, because it is part of the great natural system whereby the economy of the world is regulated and preserved. The flesh-eater triumphantly quotes Tennyson's lines in "Maud": —

> "For Nature is one with rapine, a harm no preacher can heal,
> The May-fly is torn by the swallow, the sparrow is speared by the shrike,
> And the whole little wood where I sit is a world of plunder and prey."

This being so, *"is it right,"* asks our pious and scrupulous friend *"to refuse to conform to the dictates of Nature?"*

The fallacy here consists in advancing as a binding and universal law of Nature that which is in reality only a special and partial one. It is true that *some* animals are carnivorous; if a cat were to refuse a mouse, her conduct might conceivably be argued to be unnatural, and, therefore, immoral. But it is equally true that other animals are *not* carnivorous; we are not so unreasonable as to expect a horse to eat rats and mice—why, then, should it be unnatural or ungrateful in a man to decline to prey upon the lower animals? The flesh-eater must prove that man is actually a carnivorous rather than a frugivorous being; and this, we imagine, would be rather a difficult task.

The absurd assertion so often made, that animals were *"sent"* us as food may be classed under this same head. The mere fact that we have been accustomed to eat flesh-food, no more proves that animals were created for this purpose than the existence of cannibalism proves that missionaries are "sent" to the South Sea Islands solely as an article of food, or the existence of slavery that black men were "sent" to be the slaves of white. In barbarous times cruel practices are originated, and afterwards are confirmed by centuries of habit, till at last, when humanity raises a protest against them, men are so blinded by custom as to attribute to God or nature that which is in reality only the result of their own vice and degradation.

10. The fallacy derived from *"the necessity of taking life."* Many people seem to think it a sufficient refutation of Vegetarian principles to point out that it is absolutely necessary in some cases to take the lives of animals. They delight in showing that we are obliged to kill wild animals, to keep down vermin, and to destroy domestic animals when old and diseased; or that we incidentally take life even in such innocent acts as cooking a cabbage or drinking a glass of water. The fallacy consists partly in wrongly assuming that the object of Vegetarianism is "not to take *any* life;" whereas it is really "not to take life *unnecessarily*" (the last word, conveniently omitted by our opponents, containing, in fact, the whole essence of the Vegetarian creed), and partly in the strange idea that because it is *sometimes* necessary to take life, it must be *always* allowable. Vegetarians are not so foolish as to deny the necessity of sometimes destroying animals, both intentionally and by accident; but that is no reason for killing more animals than is really necessary, but rather the reverse.[7] It is quite true that we must in self-defence keep down vermin; but it does not follow that it is advisable to eat their carcases. It is quite true that we cannot avoid accidentally taking life; but that can scarcely justify us in purposely breeding animals for the slaughter-house. To assert that because we accidentally tread on a beetle, we are justified in deliberately slaughtering an ox; or that because we chance to swallow a fly, we are right in bleeding a calf to death and enjoying our veal, is an argument which must equally justify homicide and murder of every description. A murderer might argue, in like manner, that he found he was always treading on spiders, and therefore it was obviously necessary "to take life."

---

[7] "That there is pain and evil, is no rule
That I should make it greater, like a fool."
Leigh Hunt.

11. "*The Scriptural argument.*" I have often been met by the remark that any system which condemns flesh-eating must be wrong, because it was sanctioned by the usages of the Jews, and is mentioned without disapproval in the New Testament. Having no wish to enter on any religious controversy, I will very briefly state why I consider such reasoning fallacious. It is only in late ages that Vegetarianism has been seriously studied and adopted as a principle; only lately has its deeper import been widely and systematically recognised. It follows, therefore, that it is unreasonable to look to the New Testament for teaching on this subject, which was quite unknown to the Jews of that day, and was reserved for the consideration of a future generation. Why need we fear to admit that morality, or rather the knowledge of morality, is progressive, and that which is allowable in one age is not necessarily so in another? For instance, the habit of slavery was sanctioned in the Old Testament, and not condemned in the New; yet it is not now denied that the abolition of slavery marked an advance in moral knowledge. So, too, it will be in the question of Food Reform.

I have now answered what appear to me to be the commonest of our adversaries' arguments. Would-be Vegetarians are at first so often subjected to annoyance and molestation, owing to the kindly anxieties of friends and relatives, and the more officious advice of acquaintances, that it is well to be fore-armed in argument. The early career of a Vegetarian is indeed often a veritable "Pilgrim's Progress." He meets with no lack of such characters as Mistrust, Timorous, and Ignorance: Mr. Worldly Wiseman, the representative of Society, is always at hand with his plausible remonstrances: even the dreadful Apollyon himself, in the form of the family physician, occasionally bestrides the path of the bold adventurer, with his awful and solemn warning—"Prepare thyself to die." But if the pilgrim presses boldly on his course, these early obstacles will rapidly vanish from his path; even as Apollyon, when he felt the thrust of Christian's sword, "spread forth his dragon's wings and sped him away."

SPORT.

On the 9th of May, 1884, the House of Lords discussed and rejected a bill which practically aimed at the direct abolition of pigeon shooting, though introduced under the circuitous title of the "Cruelty to Animals Act Amendment Bill." The arguments of those who supported the measure were directed chiefly to show that there is something peculiarly base and demoralising in pigeon shooting, which distinguishes it from other sport; while their antagonists contended that there is no real distinction between this and other kinds of sport, and that the proposed legislation is merely the thin end of the wedge which would finally destroy the immemorial resource and recreation of true-born English men. "If it was cruel," said the Earl of Redesdale, "to shoot at a pigeon with intent to kill it, so it was cruel to shoot at partridges and pheasants."

Now no humanitarian will be likely to desire the prolongation of pigeon-shooting merely because it is *no worse* than other shooting; by all means let the thin end of the wedge be inserted, if the butt end cannot be used for a single crushing blow. But it must be admitted that, from a logical standpoint, Lord Redesdale, and those who voted with him, had decidedly the better of their inconsistent though well-meaning opponents. The fact is that *all* sport is essentially the same in principle, and one cannot logically and rationally condemn one branch of it without condemning it as a whole. Nothing could have been more feeble than the well-meant argument of the late Archbishop of Canterbury, that pigeon-shooting "did not belong to those sports which were so dear to Englishmen, but to a class of sport which was passing out of use—that of preying on the sufferings of confined animals." For, first, it may be pertinently inquired, *how* is it more cruel to prey on the sufferings of a confined than an unconfined animal? And, secondly, even if we admit that it is more cruel, did not the Archbishop himself perpetrate the very same enormity, though not under the name of sport, when he dined that same evening, and preyed on the sufferings of some confined ox or sheep which had suffered at Deptford that he might feast at Lambeth. I think it will be found by anyone who thoroughly considers the matter, that it is exceedingly difficult, if not impossible, to find a logical standpoint for condemning the cruelty of any particular branch of slaughter as distinct from the rest; if we wish to be consistent, they must all stand or fall together.

The essence of so-called "sport" consists in the excitement derived from the pursuit and killing of animals. It seems that there are two warring instincts in men's minds—one, the brutal passion, which prompts them to pursue and slaughter innocent and helpless creatures, a passion which, unfortunately, has been so strengthened by centuries of habit, that in some persons it is engrafted like a second nature; the other, the gentler, and surely not less natural feeling, which bids us pity, sympathise, and save. I believe that this latter instinct is destined eventually to triumph over the former, and the triumph would be the speedier, were it not that certain attendant circumstances combine to throw a fictitious charm over our national field-sports, and so prevent us from realising the great cruelty that underlies them. In hunting, for instance, the most popular of all field-sports, the pleasant surroundings, the excitement of the "meet," the beauty of the country, the strength and speed of the horses, and the skill of their riders, make men forget the nature of the detestably barbarous and unmanly business for which they are met. Well does Sir Thomas More exclude hunting from the pleasures of his model people in "Utopia." "Nor can they comprehend," he says, "the pleasure of seeing dogs run after a hare more than of seeing one dog run after another; for if the seeing them run is that which gives the pleasure, you have the same entertainment to the eye on both these occasions, since that is the same in both cases; but if the pleasure lies in seeing the hare killed and torn by the dogs, this ought rather to stir pity, that a weak, harmless, and fearful hare should be devoured by strong, fierce, and cruel dogs." Such a sight ought, indeed, to stir pity and indignation; but thoughtlessness and custom can do much to banish these emotions from our minds.

Again, in the case of shooting and fishing, it is strange that English gentlemen should love to do the work which should be done (if done at all) by the butcher and fishmonger. Here too, as in hunting, the skill of the sportsman lends to the sport a seeming charm, which it would not otherwise possess. Yet the essential point of the sport does not lie in this exercise of skill, but in the fact that the animal's life is at stake. Sport is none the less sport when enjoyed by the poor man, who clumsily "pots" a blackbird, than by a noble lord, who dexterously brings down a snipe or woodcock. However brutal and degrading a habit may be, there is sure to be no lack of skill in carrying it into effect, when it once becomes systematised and established as a regular practice; but it is absurd in the highest degree to argue that *because* there is such skill, the habit itself is justifiable. The sport of bull-fighting, if introduced into England, would no doubt increase the activity and agility of those engaged in it; yet even the dullest country gentleman would protest against so detestable a custom. We read in French history that during the Huguenot and Catholic wars, when there were savage reprisals on both sides, the young nobles had become so accustomed to bloodshed, that they made a fashion of ferocity, and practised graceful ways of striking a death-blow! One can imagine how indignantly these young warriors would have repelled the notion that they were common murderers, and have shown (by an argument exactly similar to that of our modern sportsmen) that they slaughtered their victims not for the sake of killing them, but for the pleasure of graceful swordsmanship.

The excuses offered by sportsmen, in justification or palliation of their pursuit, are indeed so remarkable, and occasionally so ingenious, as to deserve special attention. We are often reminded by the writers in *Land and Water*, and other sporting journals, that field-sports are "national," and hence it is concluded that they are praiseworthy; it being conveniently ignored or forgotten that there are such things as national errors, as well as national virtues, and that the error of a nation is even more calamitous than the error of an individual. Another amusing justification of sport is that the animal has a "chance of escape," and therefore there is no cruelty; as if an agonising uncertainty were better than a speedy and merciful death! Again, it is often asserted that shooting, fishing, etc., must have a beneficial effect on the sportsman, because they bring him into contact with nature among the woods and streams. It is not to be doubted that the contact with nature must in itself be beneficial; but could it not be obtained without the slaughter of birds and fish? and can those men be true and perfect lovers of nature who frequent her paths only that they may deal death and destruction among her harmless children? The dynamiters who cross the Atlantic to blow up an English town might on this principle justify the object of their journey by the assertion that the sea-voyage brought them in contact with the exalting and ennobling influences of the Atlantic.

But the crowning absurdity of the sportsman's arguments, an absurdity which beats any of the fallacies to be found in Sydney Smith's "Noodle's Oration," is the wonderful assertion that sport lends to the character a special kind of gentleness and humanity! The true sportsman, like the true soldier, is never cruel. He is merciful, chivalrous, thoughtful, tender-hearted, sympathetic. These qualities are the result of the practice of sport. They are not (as might at first have been imagined) acquired by butchers, for the butcher's trade is not "sport;" they are the glorious possession of those unselfish individuals who devote a lifetime to hunting, shooting, and fishing. I have several times heard this plea gravely advanced as a justification of field sports, so it may be worth while to point out (with apologies to my readers for an apparent insult to their reasoning abilities) that it is not much credit to a sportsman, who systematically commits the cruelty of taking away harmless lives for his own idle recreation, to be able to urge in self-defence that he does not needlessly torture his victims. Possibly not; but what then? At best, this limitation shows that a sportsman is not quite such a ruffian as he might be. It is difficult to be serious in refuting such arrant and disingenuous nonsense, so I will conclude with a short quotation from one of De Quincey's best known books, his essay on "*Murder, considered as one of the Fine Arts.*" In this essay he humorously treats of murder—much as the sportsman affects to regard sport—as an honourable profession, giving scope to the highest art and dexterity of handiwork, and ennobling the character of those who practise it. I recommend the careful study of the following passage to those who believe in the exalting influences of sport:—

> "The subject chosen [*i.e.,* for the murderer to operate on] ought to be in good health, for it is absolutely barbarous to murder a sick person, who is usually quite unable to bear it. And here, in this benign attention to the comfort of sick people, you will observe the usual effect of a fine art to soften and refine the feelings. . . . From our art, as from all the other liberal arts, when thoroughly mastered, the result is, to humanise the heart."

Mutatis mutandis, we have here the very words of the advocates of sport. The humanity of the sportsman is, we suspect, closely akin to that of Tom

Tulliver, whom George Eliot describes in the *Mill on the Floss* as "a young gentleman fond of animals—fond, that is, of throwing stones at them."

There can be little doubt that the chief strength of sport lies, not in the ridiculous arguments often put forward by its votaries, but in the fact that the institution of the slaughter-house is still regarded by a vast majority of people as necessary and indispensable. There is, of course, a difference between killing animals for food, and that amateur slaughtering which is dignified with the title of sport: the former may conceivably be justifiable, the latter can never be so. But still there is so much similarity between the two, that it is almost impossible to get people to think of them separately. "If they were called upon to put an end to pigeon-shooting," said Earl Fortescue in the debate in the House of Lords, before alluded to, "they might next be called upon to put an end to the slaughter of live stock." They might, indeed. Those who detest cruelty will not cease to call for its abolition, in whatever form it may manifest itself. Sport is perhaps the most silly and vulgar of all forms of cruelty but we must not be surprised if it lingers on until men have learnt the folly and brutality of slaughtering animals for food. As long as animals are regarded as merely "the beasts that perish," there will be all sorts of cruelty in the way they are treated by men.

THE PHILOSOPHY OF CANNIBALISM.

Cannibalism is a subject which, though not pleasant in itself, must inevitably have some interest for those who study the food question, as marking the extreme limit of human folly and depravity in the choice of diet. It has of late been brought rather forcibly into public notice by the revelation of the terrible events connected with the Greeley Expedition and the voyage of the yacht Mignonette; but, as a rule, it is a subject on which people are rather reticent, and in the contemplation of which society does not greatly care to indulge. I confess I think this scruple on the part of our carnivorous friends rather too squeamish and sentimental, for cannibalism is not only a branch of that great flesh-eating system of diet of which they are upholders, but it is beyond doubt the most logical and fully developed realisation of the principles on which that system is based.

Cannibalism, like ordinary flesh-eating, may claim to be a time-honoured institution. We read of cannibals in the history and legendary traditions of all ages, from the ogre Polyphemus, who, as Homer tells us, devoured the companions of Ulysses, to the modern savages of New Zealand, who did not hesitate to make a hearty meal off any prisoners, captives, or missionaries whom fortune might put in their power. Some writers have questioned the deliberate practice of cannibalism, but well-attested facts[8] concerning many savage tribes leave us no room for doubt that human flesh is often used by choice as an article of diet, and not only under the pressure of necessity or from the lack of other food. It is quite possible that there is a basis of truth in the grimly humorous stories told by the old Greek historian Herodotus of the cannibals of his age, among some of whom it was the custom when a man died for his relations to assemble and eat him, mixing his flesh with that of some animal to make it more palatable. Others again used to eat their aged parents, while a third tribe, the Padœans, carried on the practice of cannibalism in a

---

[8] See especially Chapter 5 of "Hayti; or, the Black Republic," Smith, Elder, & Co., 1884.

more systematic and scientific manner. "If one of their number be ill," says Herodotus,[9] "they take the sick person, and, if he be a man, the men of his acquaintance proceed to put him to death, because, they say, his flesh would be spoilt for them if he pined and wasted away with sickness. The man protests he is not ill in the least; but his friends will not accept his denial. In spite of all he can say, they kill him and feast themselves on his body."

It is indisputable that there have been, and indeed are, savage tribes who deliberately prefer human flesh to other food; and it should not escape our notice that these people, in defence of their dietetic peculiarities, might use, and probably have used, arguments similar to those now-a-days brought forward by flesh-eaters in justification of their system of diet—"It has always been so;" "it is the regular rule of our society;" "our medical men approve of it;" "we are strong and healthy on this diet;" "it is evidently the law of Nature;" "it is much kinder to the victims than to leave them to die of a lingering old age;" "the world would be over-run with old and sick people if we did not eat them;" "it is absolutely necessary at times to take life;" "we must be practical, and not give way to humanitarian sentiment"—all these are fallacies which must surely have been employed by many a patriotic cannibal, as well as by the Englishmen who are determined to see no fault in their native beef. There is no lack of instances of a belief in the advantages of a cannibalistic diet. The Grand Khan of Tartary is said to have fattened his magicians and astronomers with the carcases of condemned criminals; on the same principle, I suppose, as our clergymen and men of science find they need plenty of butchers' meat to insure a proper fulfilment of their professional duties. Richard Cœur de Lion, according to an old English ballad, owed his recovery from a serious illness to a Turk's head, which his cook dressed for him as a substitute for pork. The Caribbees were said to prefer sucking infants to all other food, and doubtless felt all the affecting partiality for this form of diet which Charles Lamb expressed for roast sucking-pig. In fact, so many merits have been discovered, at different times and in different places, in human flesh, when used for culinary purposes, that it is to be regretted that no enterprising cannibals volunteered to open a department in the late Health Exhibition as a counterpoise to the Vegetarian dining-room, and an encouragement to flesh-eaters in general.

---

[9] Book III., chapter 99, Rawlinson's Translation.

But of late cannibalism has for some reason or other fallen into disrepute, even among those who ought logically to be numbered among its supporters. Its scientific and systematic practice is now relegated to a few barbarous nations, while Europeans, although still addicted in the main to flesh-eating, become cannibals only under the pressure of some great necessity, as in time of siege or shipwreck, and even then the utmost exertions are usually made by the survivors to keep secret the manner in which they preserved their own lives. When the fact became known that cannibalism had been practised by the survivors in the Greeley Expedition, "the public conscience," as the daily papers informed us, "was inexpressibly pained and shocked at these revelations." Now, all Food Reformers must necessarily be glad to notice any sign of the existence of a public conscience in relation to the question of food, for the principle to which flesh-eaters usually appeal is that "law of Nature" which prompts the stronger animals to prey on the weaker, and which is sometimes naively described, by a happy inversion, as "the great law of self-sacrifice." If once the public conscience can be awakened, it is possible that in time it may be 1nexpressibly pained and shocked by other things besides cannibalism, which are now established as mere every-day matters in our midst. So, without wishing to weaken the just detestation in which cannibalism is at present held, I should like to inquire a little into the reasons on which this abhorrence is based, and to see if they do not lead us to wider and fuller conclusions than those hitherto reached by well-meaning anti-cannibalistic flesh-eaters.

In what, then, does the peculiar horror of cannibalism consist? Not in the mere taking of human life, for war, the profession of killing, is everywhere held in high esteem, and it is only of late years that duelling has ceased to be equally popular. If we are thought to be justified in killing our fellow-creatures for the sake of prestige, honour, and empire, why should we be ashamed to do so for more solid dietetic advantages, if a diet of human flesh were considered wholesome and necessary? It is obvious that the popular aversion to cannibalism is based, and justly so, on the intuitive knowledge that such a diet is unnatural, unwholesome, and disgusting; the very word "cannibal," or "dog-like," is indicative of the popular sentiment. It is rightly felt that there are some foods of which it is filthy and dog-like to partake, and the public conscience is accordingly shocked when some shipwrecked individuals from time to time are found to have preferred such a diet to the alternative of starvation. On the whole, this is as it should be; but it is to be regretted that the public conscience should be so partial and intermittent in its promptings, branding as infamy the mad act of a few starving and scarcely responsible men, while it calmly ignores or sanctions an established system which outrage's every feeling of decency and humanity. For let those who shudder at the horrors of cannibalism lay aside for once all the prejudice of custom and conventionalism, and think of the real meaning of the slaughter of animals for food. Let them track the beef-steak or the mutton-chop, which they so greatly relish at lunch, first to the butcher's shop and then to the slaughter-house, and, finally, let them seriously consider whether the upholders of such a system are justified in expressing any virtuous horror at the diet of which cannibals partake. They may call their butcher a "purveyor" and his slaughter-house an "abattoir," but they cannot evade the fact that their own daily food is in its substance disgusting, and procured by a process which is loathsome to all the finer instincts of their mind.

It is said that the Papuan inhabitants of New Britain are accustomed to expose human flesh for sale in their shops and markets. This, if true, is certainly very sad and terrible, but it is even more sad and undeniably true, that the people of *old* Britain look with perfect composure and satisfaction on the horrible array of dangling limbs and quartered carcases which is everywhere to be seen along the main thoroughfares of the most civilised towns. If we wish to see cannibalism (in its literal sense) rampant and unchecked, we need not go very far from home to enjoy this instructive spectacle, for the roast beef of Old England, as well as the roast man of New Britain, will supply a fruitful subject of meditation to those who deplore that dog-like perversity of appetite which prompts men to glut themselves with food at once disgusting and degrading, while they neglect or despise the pure and simple gifts scattered everywhere by the bountiful hand of Nature.

VEGETARIANISM AND SOCIAL REFORM.

There are many signs that what has very properly been called the "Great Food Question" will soon be recognised as a subject of immediate and paramount importance. The surface of party politics may be agitated by the fortunes of this or that legislative proposal, but the question which will chiefly occupy the minds of thoughtful men is how a sufficient food supply is to be provided for the increasing millions of the nation, and how we are to meet the social crisis which seems to be impending at no distant date, owing to the terrible destitution of the lower classes. Many are the suggestions constantly being put forward for the solution of this great national problem, but most of them are sadly inadequate and insufficient. Emigration is the favourite remedy of a certain class of economists and politicians, but, apart from the objections to the injustice of this scheme, which would enforce an unwelcome exile on large masses of Englishmen, there seems to be no certainty that it would really improve the condition of those who remain in England. The Malthusians, again, would have us believe that things can never come right until a limit is put to the numbers of families; but though this doctrine finds favour with high economic writers, it is one which the good feeling of the nation naturally and intuitively rejects. So urgent is the need of some remedial scheme, that certain writers have even detected the future salvation of England in what is known as the "freezing process," by which the carcases of sheep are preserved in the antipodes, and brought to our shores in floating mortuaries constructed for that purpose. In the absence of more practical plans of relief than those I have mentioned, it is not to be wondered that the supporters of thorough social reform boldly assert that nothing short of direct legislative action can materially benefit the condition of our English poor.

What have we Vegetarians to say on this subject, and what part can we claim to play in the solution of this great question? In my opinion, it is important that we should ponder our position thoughtfully, and be careful to claim what is really our due—neither too much nor too little. It is admitted on all hands that a fleshless diet effects an enormous economic saving, and it is not seriously denied that such a diet is perfectly practicable for those who choose to try it. What, then, will be the value of Vegetarianism at a time when the nation 1s racking its brains to find methods of feeding its millions, who at present, from some reason or other, are woefully short of food?

In the first place, I think we shall do wisely in not claiming too much. The unhappy condition of the lower classes is brought about by many complex causes, which can scarcely be remedied by any single reform. The evil lies in the inequality of the laws which regulate the distribution of wealth, rather than in any actual dearth of means of subsistence. It may therefore be fairly questioned whether, to gain a final and permanent relief, it would not be necessary to go beyond individual food-thrift, and to place the whole system of the production of wealth on a really equitable basis.[10]

On the other hand, we must not fail to claim for our system the immense importance to which it is justly entitled. Though Vegetarianism may not be the *only* reform that is needed, it is none the less true that no other reform, without it, can be really and permanently successful. A nation that does not appreciate the value of food-thrift can never be really prosperous. The unjust influence of the wealthy classes may be curtailed by legislation, but the life of the people will never be really happy unless they have learned to practise frugality and simplicity of diet. Great, too, is the indirect influence of Vegetarian principles in the carrying out of any plan of social reform. A pure and enlightened system of diet almost of necessity disposes the minds of those who practise 1t to general habits of simplicity and unselfishness. Those who have realised the value of moderation and economy in matters of food and

---

[10] It is often asserted by Socialists that the adoption of a thrifty diet could not in itself improve the condition of the poor to any large extent. Individuals, they say, may at present save largely by the economy of a vegetable diet, but when once the possibility of such a diet began to be recognised, wages would fall in proportion, and the whole advantage of the thrift would go to the capitalist class. This is very strongly urged by Mr. George in *Progress and Poverty*, Book VI., Chapter I.; and the obvious inference is that some external legislative change has, in the present state of affairs, become an absolute necessity. But while making this admission all Food Reformers must protest against the very slight importance attributed by Mr. George to habits of thrift and frugality in living. However true it may be that such self-reform is of itself useless, in the face of the constant pressure of poverty caused by insufficient wages, it is nevertheless deplorably unwise to undervalue and decry the importance of habits without which no community can ever live in true happiness and content.

drink are not likely to look with a favourable eye on vast accumulations of private wealth, contrasted with an appalling destitution among other classes of their fellow-countrymen. The Vegetarian, who recognises in the earth the common mother whose kindly fruits are scattered in abundance before us all, can scarcely desire to see the land, the source of all life and all wealth, otherwise than the property of the nation that dwells upon it.

One not unfrequently hears food-thrift decried by ardent social reformers for the reasons I have indicated above. More careful consideration would have enabled them to see that no true reforms can be really incompatible or antagonistic. The well-being of a nation, which is the aim and object of the schemes of all wise reformers, cannot be effected by the single operation of any one remedy, but will be the outcome of the harmonious working of all. Each reform contributes in its own sphere to the realisation of the whole, and, in its own way, is absolutely indispensable. There are many such movements at present going on among us; but none is more valuable and necessary than the reform of diet.